I Hate Everything.

THIS JOURNAL BELONGS TO

I Hate Everything.

THE JOURNAL YOU HATE TO WRITE IN.

Matthew DiBenedetti

Avon, Massachusetts

Contains material adapted and abridged from *I Hate
Everything.* by Matthew DiBenedetti, copyright © 2010 by
Matthew DiBenedetti, ISBN 10: 1-4405-0638-8, ISBN 13:
978-1-4405-0638-3.

Published by Adams Media,
a division of F+W Media, Inc.
57 Littlefield Street,
Avon, MA 02322. U.S.A.
www.adamsmedia.com

Interior illustrations and design by Elisabeth Lariviere
Cover design by Frank Rivera and Jessica Faria

ISBN 10: 1-4405-2862-4
ISBN 13: 978-1-4405-2862-0

Printed in the United States of America.

10   9   8   7   6   5   4   3   2   1

*This book is available at quantity discounts for bulk purchases.
For information, please call 1-800-289-0963.*

I hate everything.

And, I know I'm not alone. One day, I just started jotting down all the things that I hated and couldn't believe how many things there were that I truly disliked. If you are like me and hate everything too, then you'll know what to do in the journal pages that follow . . .

MATTHEW

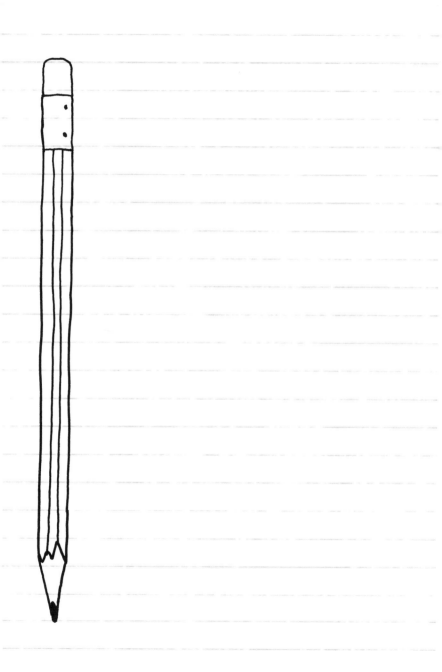

I hate when people use pencils.
(There's no going back and erasing when you hate everything!)

I hate kitten calendars.

THINGS I HATE TODAY . . .

        /   /

THINGS I HATE THAT START WITH THE LETTER M . . .

I hate meaningless Facebook posts.

I hate that you think I care what you're doing right now.

I hate that I don't have more Friends.

EVERYTHING I HATE TODAY ...

/   /

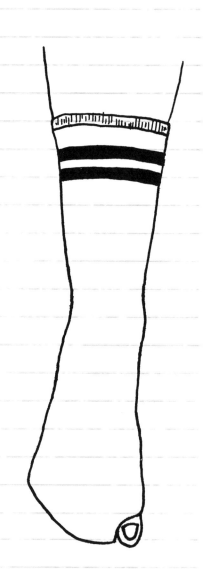

I HATE THESE SONGS . . .

I hate songs that bring back memories.

WHAT I HATE TODAY . . .

/   /

THINGS THAT I HATE TO DO . . .

THINGS I HATE TODAY . . .

/   /

I hate living with someone.

I hate being alone.

THINGS I HATE THAT START WITH THE LETTER F...

I hate that if it's not on a list, I forget.
I hate lists.

-
-
-
-
-
-
-
-
-
-
-
-
-
-
-
-

I HATE THAT THESE PEOPLE HAVEN'T BEEN ABDUCTED BY ALIENS . . .

EVERYTHING I HATE TODAY . . .

/   /

I HATE THAT I HAVE NOT PLAYED SPIN THE BOTTLE
WITH . . .

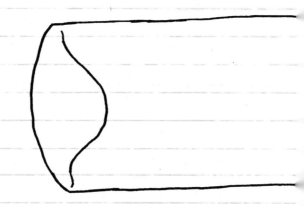

I HATE THAT I HAVE PLAYED WITH . . .

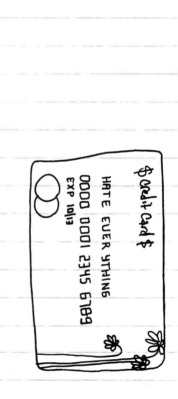

WHAT I HATE TODAY . . .

/ /

I hate wasting space.

I hate wasting time.

I hate that the only good part
of an artichoke is the heart.

I hate that my heart is an open book.

I HATE THE TASTE OF . . .

I hate when milk goes bad.

THINGS I HATE TODAY . . .

/   /

I hate coloring between the lines.

THINGS I HATE THAT START WITH THE LETTER S . . .

I hate playing by the rules.

Everything I hate today . . .

/   /

I hate movies that don't have happy endings.

Movies I hate . . .

WHAT I hate TODAY . . .

/   /

THINGS I HATE ABOUT MY EX . . .

I hate running into exes.
I hate that the only good times with an ex
were the day we met and the day we broke up.
I hate speed bumps.

I hate that we all just can't get along.

THINGS I HATE TODAY . . .

/   /

THINGS I HATE THAT START WITH THE LETTER B . . .

I hate that my bellybutton no longer has a purpose.

EVERYTHING I HATE TODAY . . .

/   /

I hate feeling obligated to look at people's photo albums.

I HATE WHEN PEOPLE . . .

I hate seeing people pick their nose while driving.

I hate that there really isn't a safe place to pick your nose.

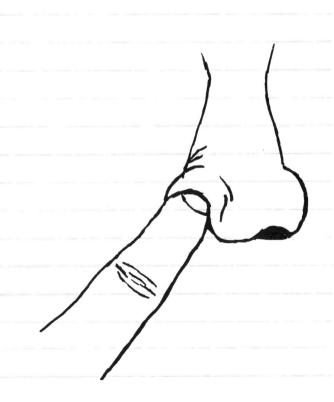

WHAT I HATE TODAY . . .
/   /

I HATE THAT THESE THINGS KEEP ME UP AT NIGHT . . .

I hate the saying "don't let the bedbugs bite."
I hate knowing bedbugs exist.

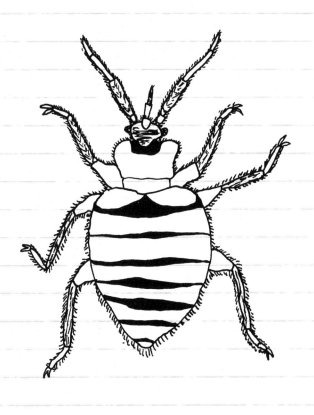

THINGS I HATE TODAY . . .

/   /

THINGS I HATE THAT START WITH THE LETTER T . . .

EVERYTHING I HATE TODAY . . .

/   /

I hate that one person can make a difference.

I hate that I'm not that person.

I hate that I don't know that person.

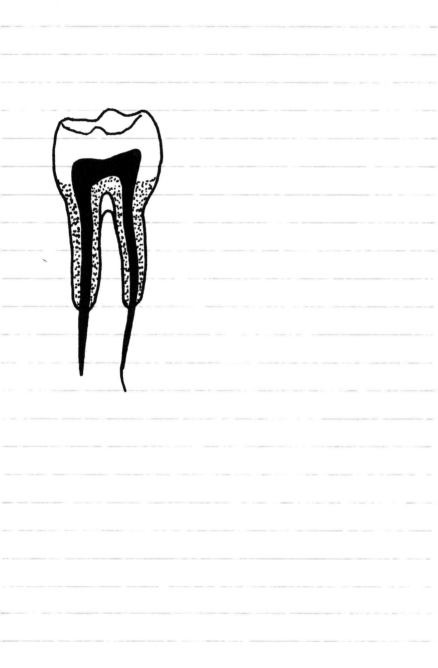

Places I Hate to Go . . .

WHAT I HATE TODAY . . .

/   /

I HATE THAT I CAN'T DO THIS BETTER . . .

I hate that the Force is not strong with me.

THINGS I HATE TODAY . . .

/   /

THINGS I HATE THAT START WITH THE LETTER M...

I hate those strands of hair that cling to the shower wall.

EVERYTHING I HATE TODAY . . .

/ /

THINGS I HATE ABOUT THE HOLIDAYS . . .

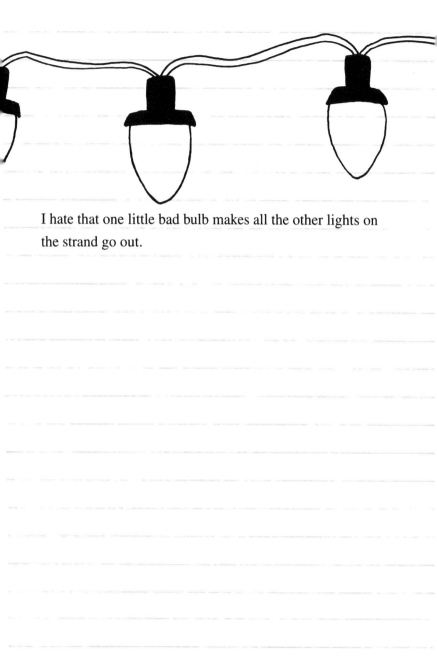

I hate that one little bad bulb makes all the other lights on the strand go out.

WHAT I HATE TODAY . . .
            /   /

THINGS I HATE TO TOUCH . . .

THINGS I HATE TODAY . . .

      /   /

THINGS I HATE THAT START WITH THE LETTER P . . .

I hate that I have to keep changing my password.

new password | ********** |

re-enter password | **********| |

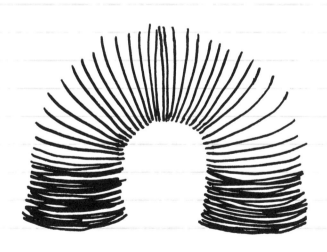

I hate when Slinkies go bad.

EVERYTHING I HATE TODAY . . .

/   /

THINGS I HATE BUYING . . .

I hate getting things started.

I hate that I've never really finished anythi

I hate that I've never discovered dinosaur bones.

I HATE THAT I'VE NEVER . . .

WHAT I HATE TODAY . . .

        /   /

THINGS I HATE THAT START WITH THE LETTER K . . .

I hate kids.

THINGS I HATE TODAY . . .

/   /

NAMES THAT I HATE . . .

I hate trendy kid names.

EVERYTHING I HATE TODAY . . .

/   /

THINGS I HATE ABOUT BEING THIS OLD . . .

ELLIE
AGE 8

JOHNNY
AGE 8

JOHNNY
AGE 7

ELLIE
AGE 7

JOHNNY
AGE 6

ELLIE
AGE 6

ELLIE-AGE 5

JOHNNY
AGE 5

ELLIE
AGE 4

I hate that they grow up so fast.

I hate that we do too.

JOHNNY
AGE 4

WHAT I HATE TODAY . . .

/   /

THINGS I HATE THAT START WITH THE LETTER A . . .

THINGS I HATE TODAY . . .

/   /

I HATE GETTING GROSSED OUT BY . . .

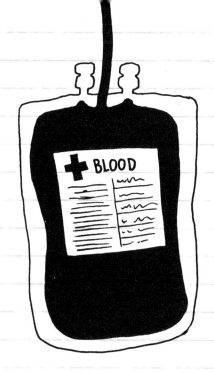

I hate that blood makes me queasy.

I hate that I don't have more blood to donate.

THE TOP THINGS I HATE THAT ARE WORTH
SHARING WITH OTHERS . . .

I'd hate if anyone found out I hated these things.

EVERYTHING I HATE TODAY . . .

/   /

I hate that there are so many things to hate.

I hate negativity.

I hate that I hate all these things too.

If it wasn't for what I hate about this . . .

(I might actually like something.)

The one thing that I hate most of all . . .

I HATE THAT I NEED A BIGGER JOURNAL FOR EVERY-
THING I HATE.

So Much More to Hate

P.S. . . . I hate postscripts.

If you're craving more loathing, you can keep the hates coming or share some hates of your own by proudly joining the many people like you on . . .

Facebook: I HATE EVERYTHING
Twitter: WhatIHateToday
www.TheHatePage.com

And look for the original book, *I Hate Everything.*, as well as the daily calendar, in all major bookstores and online retailers.

I'd hate it if you missed out on any of the fun of hating!